UNLEASH JOY
WORKBOOK
&
JOURNAL

My Journey Began on:

JOURNALING IS LIKE
WHISPERING TO ONESELF
AND LISTENING AT THE SAME TIME.

MINA MURRAY, DRACULA

Unleash Joy

Welcome, bright spirit!

Inside this workbook you will find over 30 exercises, transformational questions, and mindful adult coloring (print version only) designed to enhance your reading of Unleash Joy: 30 Days to Clarity, Peace, and Long-Awaited Happiness. Some pages are designed to be utilized over and over again. I have provided a free .pdf dowload of the workbook on UnleashJoy.com/workbook so that you may print extra copies of any of the pages you find helpful.

If you've enjoyed the workbook, it would be an honor to receive a review from you on Amazon! Your review would allow me to reach more transformationally-minded women and share my path to joy with them.

Thank you so much for choosing to Unleash Joy!

Janeen

*Unattributed quotes from the book Unleash Joy: 30 Days to Clarity, Peace, and Long-Awaited Happiness

Copyright & Permissions

About Me: I'm an author, speaker and coach, specializing in helping women be transformational goddesses.
Let me be YOUR personal mastermind besty!

facebook.com/janeenrbrown
instagram.com/unleash_joy
twitter.com/JaneenBrown

Habits

I made all the choices that brought me to this moment.

Day 1: Keeping it Real

The beginning is always the hardest part; the first weight lifted, the first step in the marathon, the moment the baby is born. We're going to jump right in, and uncover some hard truths about your situation, then learn some encouraging news about the future. Let's begin, shall we?

Take a moment to look at your life with the BRAVE perspective that YOU have created it.

What experiences, situations, people, or things do you have around you that are the result of poor choices?

Which ones are the results of good choices you've made, or accomplishments you have achieved?

When you admit that your life is your own, and you accept that your situation is your own doing, you will begin to see a path that has the potential to change the things that do not bring you joy. You realize that while you may have made poor choices in the past, you can accept those choices, learn from them, and finally begin to move on.

"Until I took responsibility for my choices, I couldn't hope to make better ones."

Looking back upon your past, without judgement, or emotion, recall moments of lapsed judgement. Take this time now to recall those moments so that you may learn from those experiences.

With this insight, you can design your future self. Envision yourself with a certain credo, an internal power and wisdom that you're able to share with others. Describe her here:

"Taking responsibility is as simple as looking around, and admitting that "This is mine. I made this. I encouraged this behavior. I created this space."

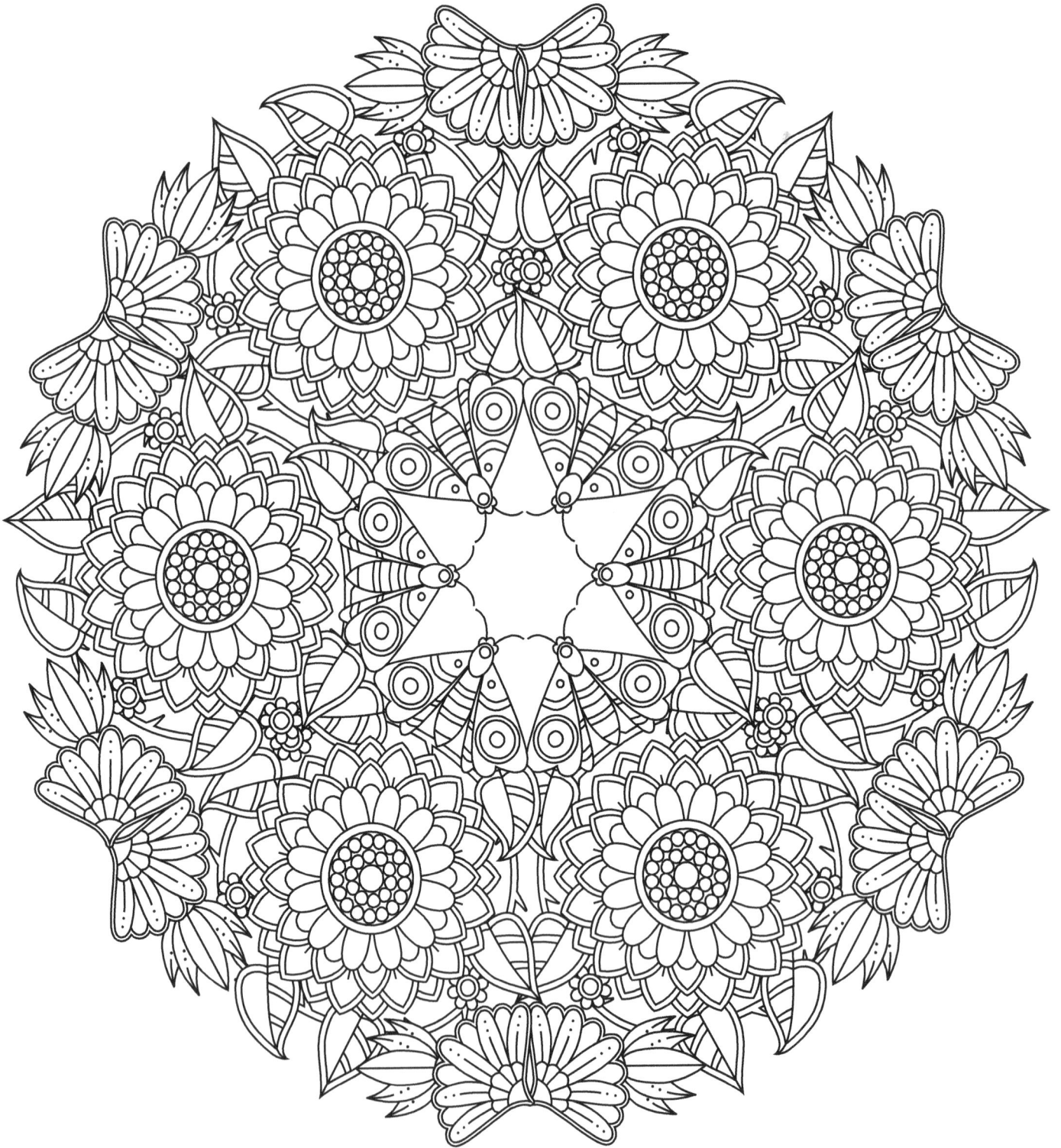

A simple smile can spread
like wildfire!

Day 2: Greet The Day

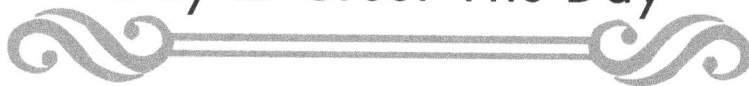

"Feeling comfortable in your skin, always caring for your body and doing your best to maintain this miraculous machine that holds your soul, is a way to tell yourself that you're worthy of health!"

Good Morning! Talking about personal responsibility is a bit "heavy". Why don't we take it easy today and just focus on feeling **good**.

Do a bit of stretching to warm up your body, increase some blood flow, and wake up! Don't worry if you are journaling at a different part of the day. Stretching is awesome any time! Now you'll be fully prepared to start tomorrow without excuses!

I stretched from my head to my toes. ☐

The next one is an easy one. You don't even have to go outside (although it's a bit nicer if the weather's cooperating)! Just get yourself to a window and stick your face in the sunshine for a moment or two. Feel the heat of it, with your eyes closed. Allow the light from that celestial source to fill your entire being. Imagine the light to be healing and energizing!

I got some sunlight on my skin. ☐

Many studies have shown that babies prefer smiling faces. A recent study in France at the University of Grenoble-Alps showed that this is particularly true for female caregivers of infants. We're born wanting our mommies to smile at us! While we certainly have no need to smile for the benefit of others, it is undeniable that smiling helps us. So smile as much as possible today, for YOU!

I smiled at myself in the mirror today. ☐

Since the 1800's psychologists have recorded evidence that your facial muscles are not only a result of, but also **a contributing factor to**, your emotional state. Smiling at yourself in the mirror several times a day can be a huge boost to confidence, a reduction in stress, and a powerful coping mechanism!

Describe the day you are creating today:

I wake up, and I am thankful.

Day 3: Give Thanks

"The one thing you always have control over is your attitude!"

Stretched ☐ Sunlight ☐ Smiled ☐

Set your intention for the day:

I am so proud of you! Today is going to be fun!! Gratitude is one of my favorite exercises. It just *feels* good. I remember thinking that this simple practice couldn't possibly make any kind of difference in the way I felt on a daily basis. I was wrong. It only took a few attempts to help me to see that gratitude would change my life for the better. It's made a difference in my relationships, the way I feel about my goals and dreams, and my attitude toward myself. I can't wait to hear about your experiences! Let's get started...

Write a list of things you are thankful for right now. Start with the simplest thing you can think of. "I love the first sip of coffee in the morning.", "Indoor plumbing rocks!", "My loved ones.", or "Pocket banana-gun holsters", or "When strangers wave at me and then realize they thought I was someone else, but I've already waved back!"

"Gratitude is the secret ingredient to happy living."

I get my torch running task out
of the way, so I can get on
with the REST of my day.

Day 4: Your Torch Running Task

"If you imagine all your tasks as small steps toward great achievement, each representative of effort, of importance, and your time's effectiveness, you can clearly see that one job outshines the others, or must be done first. That is your Torch Running Task."

Stretched ☐　Sunlight ☐　Smiled ☐

Set your intention for the day:

To Do Today:

My Torch Running Task

I Express Gratitude

❶

❷

❸

How can implementing the concept of the Torch Running Task change your level of productivity?

What one thing do you hope to accomplish in the coming week, month, or year, whilst implementing your Torch Running Task? "A year from now you'll wish you had started today." Karen Lamb

"We are what we repeatedly do. Excellence, then, is not an act, but a habit."
Will Durant

I can't change the past,
but I can choose who I
am today.

Day 5: Goal Setting

"You can't ignore the elephant in the room, when that elephant is your dream come true, just waiting around the corner for you to get up and take action."

Stretched ☐   Sunlight ☐   Smiled ☐

Set your intention for the day:

To Do Today:

My Torch Running Task

I Express Gratitude

❶

❷

❸

What do I want?

This is going to be a big day; the biggest we've had yet! Today I'm going to ask you some very important questions, in order to get to the heart of why you're here. Who are you? What do you want? Why did you choose NOW to come into this world and participate in humanity? What are you here to give?

It's ok if you don't have the answer to those questions right now. We'll find them together. The first step is to take a quiet moment to take a few deep breaths, and get comfortable, present, and grounded.

Breathe with me here: In....and out....
Relax your neck and shoulders.
Take a moment with your eyes closed to just focus on relaxing your mind and body, to breathe deeply, and to connect with the process you're about to experience.

Now, ask yourself "What do I want?" List your desires over the following pages. Use additional paper if you like, and just keep going. Don't judge your responses, instead let them flow out of you freely, without hesitation. Think of feelings, places to visit, and material things. Imagine relationships, experiences, and how you will feel at the end of it all when it's time for you to say goodbye. Write it all down.

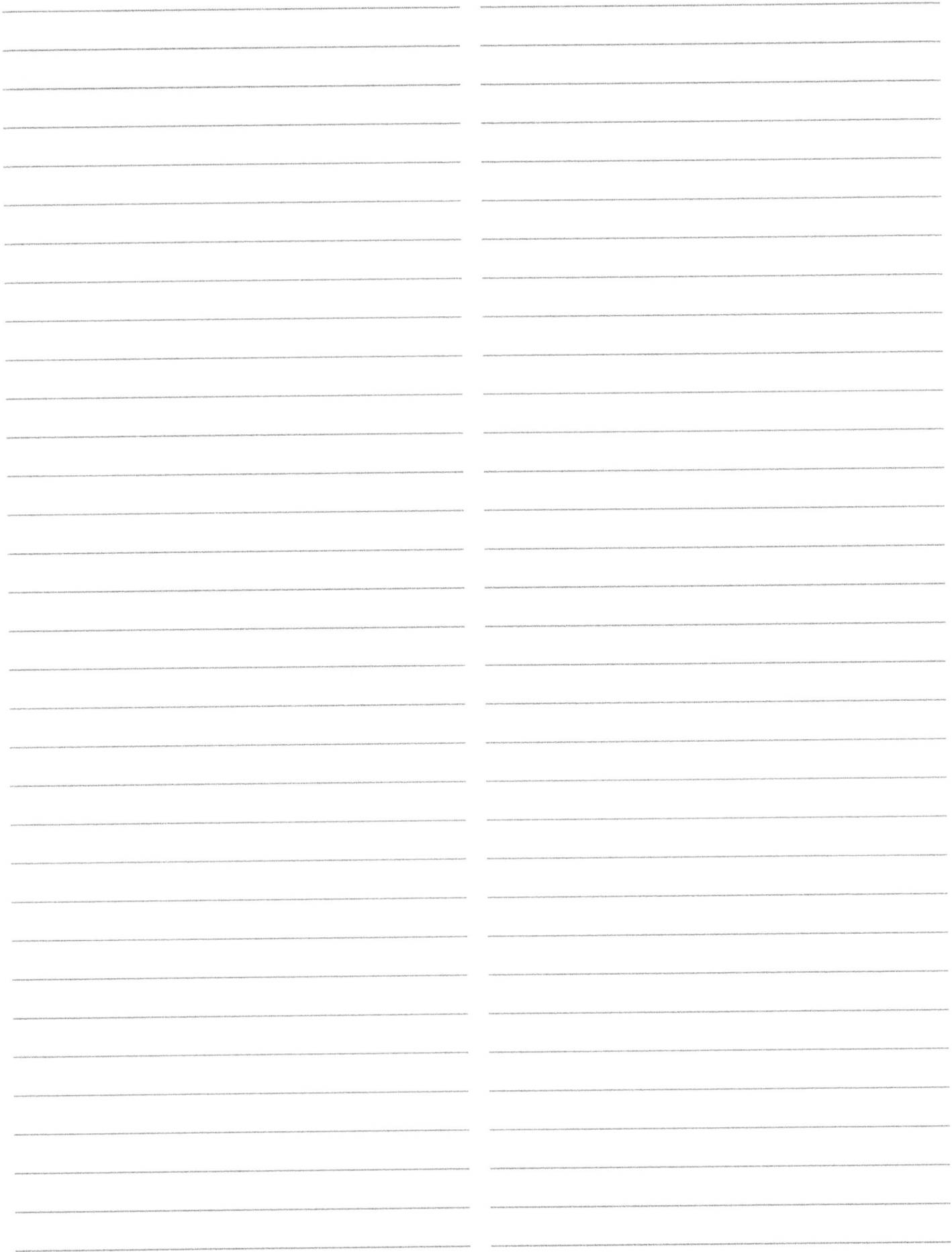

Your Life Purpose in ⑤ minutes!

Watch Adam Leipzig's TED talk on this method! www.UnleashJoy.com/resources

What is your name?

What is the ONE THING that you are supremely qualified to teach other people?

Who do you do it for? Who are these people?

What do they want or need?

How do they change or transform as a result of what you give them?

My Life Purpose Statement

I _____

for _____

so they can _____

_____

_____

SMART Goal Setting

What is my goal?

WHY is this goal important to me?

SMART Goal Checklist

is my goal...

Specific

Measurable

Achievable

Relevant

Time-Bound

What is needed to accomplish this goal?

Action Plan: My goal reverse-engineered

Action   Due Date

"When you take the time to ask yourself what you want for your future, without the baggage of thinking about anyone else, you'll be surprised by the depth and magnitude of what you want."

My kichen represents only love and peace. I create meals that nourish bodies and souls.

Day 6: Three Chores for a Happy Home

"I put myself wholly into cleaning the kitchen, knowing that I'm creating a space that will be a gift to my future self."

Stretched ☐   Sunlight ☐   Smiled ☐

My intention for today:

Today I am grateful for:

To Do Today:

_____
_____
_____
_____
_____
_____
_____
_____
_____
_____
_____
_____
_____

My Torch Running Task

Morning
☐ My bedroom is a peaceful haven.

All Day
☐ My bathroom represents cleanliness & safety.

Evening
☐ My clean kitchen is a gift to my future self.

"I want my kichen to represent only love and peace so that I can create meals that nourish bodies and souls."

When I plan my day, urgent things no longer take time from important things.

Day 7: Scheduling

"Scheduling is an excellent way to guarantee a focus on your goals and the things that matter most to you."

Stretched ☐ Sunlight ☐ Smiled ☐

My intention for today:

Today I am grateful for:

To Do Today:

_____
_____
_____
_____
_____
_____
_____
_____
_____
_____
_____
_____
_____
_____
_____
_____
_____

My Torch Running Task

Morning
☐ My bedroom is a peaceful haven.

All Day
☐ My bathroom represents cleanliness & safety.

Evening
☐ My clean kitchen is a gift to my future self.

"A schedule is a blessing to the whole family, reducing stress and bringing peace every hour."

Before you tackle your schedule, take a moment to determine what activities are most important to you, and which ones are your personal time wasting kryptonite!

Identify your Torch Running Task(s)

List your daily MUST DO activities:

What is the most powerful daily habit you could start today?

Which detrimental habit are you committed to eliminating?

List your time-wasting kryptonite activities

How can you make your torch running task MORE accessible and your kryptonite activities LESS accessible?

When are your regular meal times?

What are your ideal sleep and wake-up times?

How much time should you devote to keeping your living space tidy?

Will your schedule look the same every day, or will you have different priorities on the weekend?

Where in your schedule willl you need the most flexibility?

What parts of your schedule will be non-negotiable?

Take a moment to read through your answers and to mindfully visualize your ideal day. Now is the time to prepare a schedule that matches your goals and desires for your time. Remember that this is not set in stone. You'll need both a margin of time for the unexpected and a bit of personal grace for the times your schedule doesn't meet your mood, whims, or interests. Allow flexibility while striving for maximum accomplishment. The key is to balance the important and the immediate without losing momentum on your goals, nor being overwhelmed by interruptions and changes of plans. This requires diligence and flexibility.

Weekday Schedule

Morning

Torch Running Task
5:00 AM
6:00 AM
7:00 AM
8:00 AM
9:00 AM
10:00 AM
11:00 AM

Afternoon

12:00 PM
1:00 PM
2:00 PM
3:00 PM
4:00 PM
5:00 PM

Evening

6:00 PM
7:00 PM
8:00 PM
9:00 PM
10:00 PM
11:00 PM
12:00 PM

"Scheduling: taking control of your time and using it according to your plan, instead of being a slave to life's punches."

Weekend Schedule

Morning

Torch Running Task
5:00 AM
6:00 AM
7:00 AM
8:00 AM
9:00 AM
10:00 AM
11:00 AM

Afternoon

12:00 PM
1:00 PM
2:00 PM
3:00 PM
4:00 PM
5:00 PM

Evening

6:00 PM
7:00 PM
8:00 PM
9:00 PM
10:00 PM
11:00 PM
12:00 PM

"The person who plans their day doesn't feel overwhelmed, overloaded, or overworked – everything has its time, or place, and it actually gets done."

My personal space is a direct
reflection of my thoughts and
feelings on the inside.

Day 8: Declutter It All

"Our personal space is a direct reflection of our thoughts and feelings on the inside."

Stretched ☐ Sunlight ☐ Smiled ☐

My intention for today:

Today I am grateful for:

To Do Today:

My Torch Running Task

Morning
☐ My bedroom is a peaceful haven.

All Day
☐ My bathroom represents cleanliness & safety.

Evening
☐ My clean kitchen is a gift to my future self.

"You do not need to keep any material object to be happy, healthy, and whole."

Take a moment to visualize and create your ideal living space. What does it look, feel, and smell like? Be creative and have fun!

Creating our ideal space does not have to be an arduous, painful task. For most of us, it's simply letting go of a continual need to have MORE, and replacing it with the freedom to enjoy less. One of the best ways to begin the process is with a joyful visualization. I love Pinterest for it's wealth of beautiful room images. I can easily create a board and fill it will pictures of my dream kitchen in just a few minutes!

The first thing we may notice when looking at pictures of beautiful spaces is how much SPACE there actually is. We don't see clutter in Better Homes and Gardens! Clearing your space to make more room for you and your family to breathe is the first step to really loving your residence. Since we all process this transition differently, I have a couple of options for getting started for you:

Option A: The Clean Sweep

Remove everything from the room or area you are working on. Clean it thoroughly, then begin putting objects back carefully and considerately. Only put back the things you absolutely love, that add functionality to the space, or that you use regularly. Anything you no longer love, or that no longer serves you, can be let go of in the method of your choosing.

Option B: Kon Mari Method

Marie Kondo's book has taken the world by storm. Her simple method of gathering all related items together, asking if they spark joy, and then focusing on truly caring for your possessions has resonated with a lot of people. If this holistic style appeals to you, I recommend her book, The Lifechanging Magic of Tidying Up, and accompanying app.

Option C: Flylady

This friendly Southern gal can take you through a step-by-step process of not only de-cluttering but keeping your home clean with routines and friendly support. I highly recommend her book, Sink Reflections (the audio version is darling) and app.

See www.UnleashJoy.com/resources for easy links to these products

Room:

Areas

_____ _____
_____ _____
_____ _____
_____ _____
_____ _____
_____ _____
_____ _____

To Do

M

T

W

T

F

S

S

Cultivating strong and valuable relationships is an integral key to my success and fulfillment.

Day 9: Your Inner Circle

"Your income, your mindset, and your emotional health, are all impacted by the people around you."

Stretched ☐ Sunlight ☐ Smiled ☐

My intention for today:

Today I am grateful for:

To Do Today:

_____
_____
_____
_____
_____
_____
_____
_____
_____
_____
_____
_____
_____
_____

My Torch Running Task

Morning
☐ My bedroom is a peaceful haven.

All Day
☐ My bathroom represents cleanliness & safety.

Evening
☐ My clean kitchen is a gift to my future self.

"The people you spend the most time with affect nearly everything in your life."

"It is imperative that you surround yourself with positive, upbeat, energetic DOERS."

Person's Name:

How they influence me:

Supporter ☐ Motivator ☐ Empathizer ☐ Realist ☐ Negative Nancy ☐

Person's Name:

How they influence me:

Supporter ☐ Motivator ☐ Empathizer ☐ Realist ☐ Negative Nancy ☐

Person's Name:

How they influence me:

Supporter ☐ Motivator ☐ Empathizer ☐ Realist ☐ Negative Nancy ☐

Person's Name:

How they influence me:

Supporter ☐ Motivator ☐ Empathizer ☐ Realist ☐ Negative Nancy ☐

Person's Name:

How they influence me:

Supporter ☐ Motivator ☐ Empathizer ☐ Realist ☐ Negative Nancy ☐

Reach Out

Who do you know that lives locally, that could challenge you to become a better version of yourself?

When will you reach out to this person to arrange a meeting, coffee date, or coaching session?

What local groups or meetups can you attend to further push you toward your goals, and to network with others of like mind?

Fangirl

Who are the influencers and leaders in your field?

How can you spend more "time" with these influencers?

What books, podcasts, blogs, email lists, or groups, can you consume?

I am formulating an inner circle of people that are going to challenge me to be a greater version of myself.

Day 10: Relationships

Stretched ☐ Sunlight ☐ Smiled ☐

My intention for today:

Today I am grateful for:

To Do Today:

_____
_____
_____
_____
_____
_____
_____
_____
_____
_____
_____
_____
_____
_____

My Torch Running Task

Morning
☐ My bedroom is a peaceful haven.

All Day
☐ My bathroom represents cleanliness & safety.

Evening
☐ My clean kitchen is a gift to my future self.

I will reach out to the following individual for networking, friendship, or mentoring:

"There is no better way to build a friendship or a relationship than to show genuine interest in another person and their interests."

Someone special I will focus on today is:

This person is a:

Lover ☐　　　Child ☐　　　Friend ☐　　　Mentor ☐　　　Influencer ☐

What does this person enjoy? What makes them tick?

What are their hobbies?

What are their dreams or goals?

How may I serve or help them?

How can I be a better friend, parter, etc. to them?

Mindset

I have all the support and creativity I need to achieve financial success.

Day 11: Poverty to Abundance

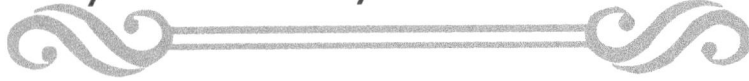

Stretched ☐ Sunlight ☐ Smiled ☐

My intention for today:

Today I am grateful for:

To Do Today:

My Torch Running Task

Morning
☐ My bedroom is a peaceful haven.

All Day
☐ My bathroom represents cleanliness & safety.

Evening
☐ My clean kitchen is a gift to my future self.

I will reach out to the following individual for networking, friendship, or mentoring:

"Believing there is enough wealth for everyone, that you are deserving of financial freedom, and feeling truly happy for others' success, is key to achieving prosperity yourself."

Take a deep breath. Changing your mindset or paradigm is a vast undertaking. Take your time examining your feelings and developing the personal belief system that brings you the most joy.

Describe your current wealth mindset? Is money easy to acquire? Do you deserve to be wealthy?

Do you have a savings account or investments? Why or why not?

What are your financial goals for you, your family, and your legacy?

Have you ever thought of your financial status as a foundation and example for future family generations?

If you could speak to your great-grandchild about your current financial status, what would you say?

What financial goals do you have for the next five years?

What investment opportunities are you interested in, or would like to learn more about?

Where can you look to learn more about financial freedom or passive income?

What skills do you already have, that you can utilize to earn income for investments?

What habits do you need to eliminate, to ensure that you live within your means?

What habits can you create, to enable you to live in your ideal financial situation?

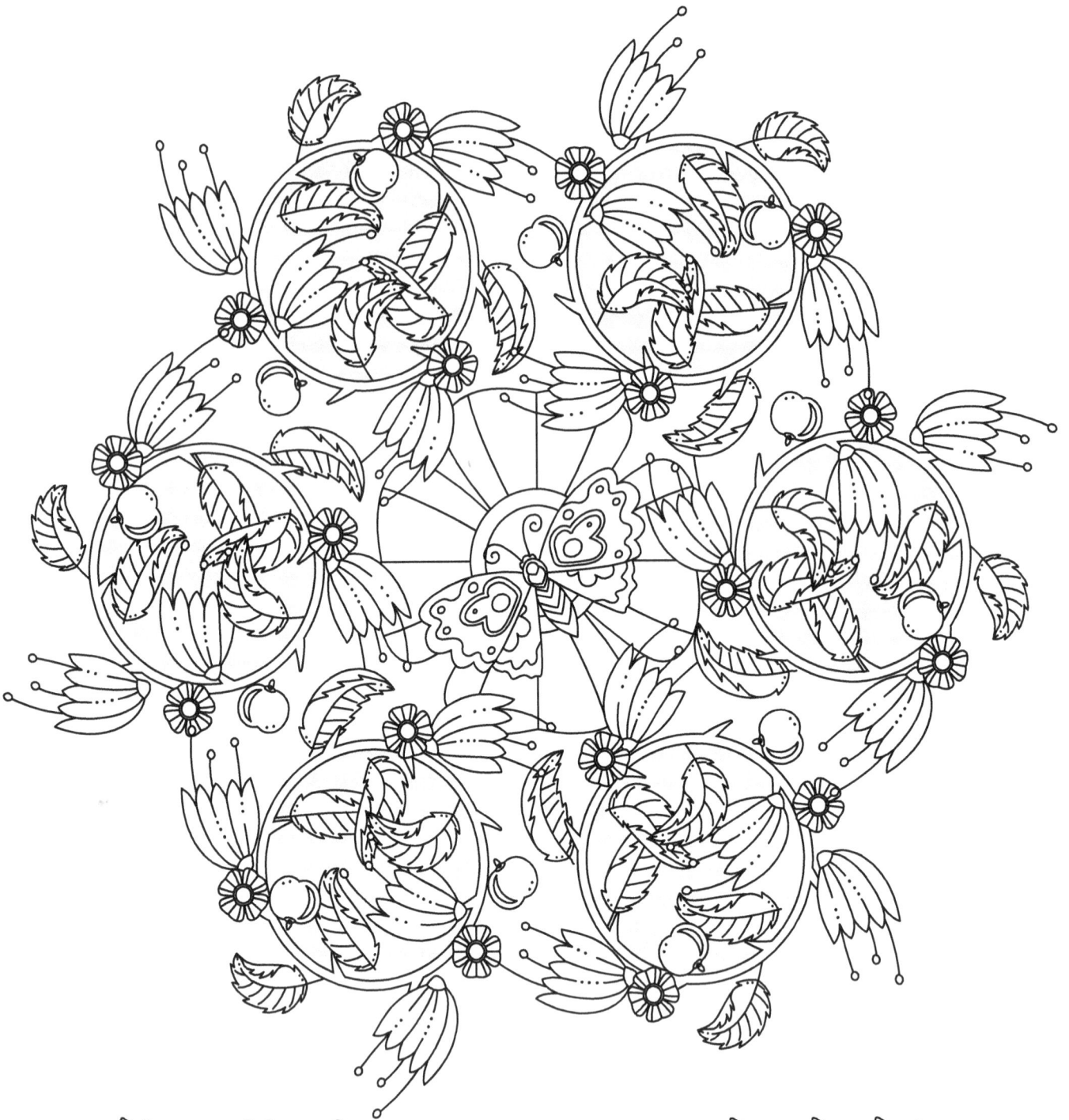

Mindfulness is: simply taking care of me, while slowing down and bringing my mind to a pure state of just being.

Day 12: Stress to Mindfulness

Stretched ☐ Sunlight ☐ Smiled ☐

My intention for today:

Today I am grateful for:

To Do Today:

_____
_____
_____
_____
_____
_____
_____
_____
_____
_____
_____
_____
_____
_____

My Torch Running Task

Morning
☐ My bedroom is a peaceful haven.

All Day
☐ My bathroom represents cleanliness & safety.

Evening
☐ My clean kitchen is a gift to my future self.

I will reach out to the following individual for networking, friendship, or mentoring:

My current financial goal & habit:

We have all had at least one experience where we reacted poorly in a given situation. You may have gotten angry or defensive and said something you shouldn't have. Perhaps you've felt rejected or attacked unnecessarily due to your assumptions. Or, you may have become hurt or offended because of something someone said or posted on social media. Poor reactions may have come from childhood trauma, angry parents, or bad examples, but because the past is done and gone, you must not use it to define yourself any longer. Your future is in your hands. The person you will become is a result of the choices you make today!

Think of a situation in which you reacted without thinking. Describe your reaction, its trigger, and how it made you feel afterward.

If you could go back in time and change your reaction, how would you react differently? How might this difference change the situation?

What are your go-to negative emotions?

What places, situations, people, or things trigger these negative emotions?

My Triggers

"When you react poorly to a situation, you train your brain to enjoy the adrenaline rush, and the negative feelings like panic, anger, frustration, and rage."

The best way to change our default-negative emotions, is to get to know them well. Understanding your nature is the first step in changing it! Take a look at those things that trigger your emotions. Work through the process of changing your default reaction to those people or events. Think of ways to remove yourself from the situation, or solve the problem.

1. Identify one of your triggers
2. Describe how this triggers a certain emotion, and why your reaction is negative.
3. Ask yourself how you can change the situation, change your reaction, or eliminate this particular trigger's influence on you. Can you change jobs, buy your coffee somewhere else, confront this person about the conflict?
4. Write an affirmation changing your default emotion into a positive one (e.g., "When I get a wrong order at a restaurant, I will take a deep breath, express gratitude by reminding myself that I am lucky to live in a time and place with an abundance of food, and empathize with the food-service worker who might have untold challenges in their life which contributed to their mistake.")
5. Visualize your positive reaction and read your affirmation daily.

My Trigger:

Why it bugs me and how it makes me feel:

What I can do to change the situation:

My positive affirmation/visualization:

"Our response to any given situation, is what really affects the outcome."

I learn by exercising my ability to seek the truth.

Day 13: Confirmation Bias to Mindful Awareness

Stretched ☐ Sunlight ☐ Smiled ☐

My intention for today:

Today I am grateful for:

☐ Today, I will be mindfully aware of things that trigger negative reactions from me.

To Do Today:

My Torch Running Task

Morning
☐ My bedroom is a peaceful haven.

All Day
☐ My bathroom represents cleanliness & safety.

Evening
☐ My clean kitchen is a gift to my future self.

I will reach out to the following individual for networking, friendship, or mentoring:

My current financial goal & habit:

I react to challenges with empathy, grace, love, and peace.

What political opinions or causes are most important to you?

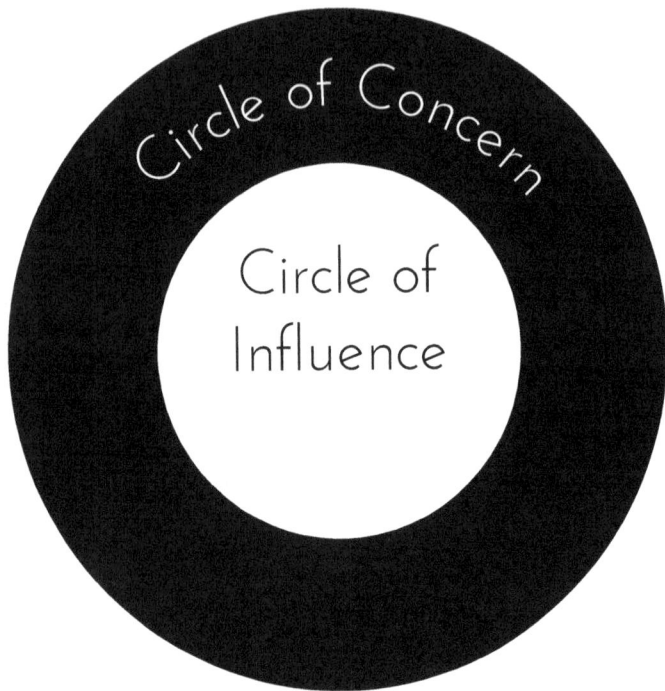

Circle of Concern

Circle of
Influence

Do these issues fall within your
circle of concern, or your circle of
influence?

In what ways can you act immediately upon the issues that concern
you?

After acting immediately, strive to set the issues aside. How can you
utilize your energy and time, toward something that brings you joy
instead?

Political Clarity

One of the most powerful life changes you can make toward joy is to completely and utterly step away from political discourse. If this is too difficult or uncomfortable, the *next* best thing is achieving clarity in your viewpoint, and cultivating wisdom and understanding of opposing oppinions.

Having such strong opinions that we are unable to have empathy or understanding for another viewpoint can be detrimental to relationships, as well as set us up for pain and regret, should we discover later that we are incorrect. Being able to view an issue from all sides, and formulate an opinion based on varied sources of information, can ensure that we not only understand opposing viewpoints, but it can also solidify and justify our own stance.

Choose one political issue that is important to you:

List three sources for information (sources that lack your already-held bias) on the opposing opinion. Consume information from these sources until you feel you have a balanced viewpoint on the subject, and a full understanding of both sides.

❶
❷
❸

Identify the opposing opinion for this issue:

☐ Start a conversation today that revolves around something joyful. Be mindful of your topics of conversation.

"Great minds discuss ideas;
Average minds discuss events;
Small minds discuss people."
Henry Thomas Buckle

My desire to improve myself, to learn, and to grow is evergreen.

Day 14: Blissfully Unaware to Empowered Action

Stretched ☐ Sunlight ☐ Smiled ☐

My intention for today:

Today I am grateful for:

☐ Today, I will be mindfully aware of things that trigger negative reactions from me.

To Do Today:

_____
_____
_____
_____
_____
_____
_____
_____
_____
_____
_____
_____
_____

My Torch Running Task

Morning
☐ My bedroom is a peaceful haven.

All Day
☐ My bathroom represents cleanliness & safety.

Evening
☐ My clean kitchen is a gift to my future self.

I will reach out to the following individual for networking, friendship, or mentoring:

My current financial goal & habit:

"Feedback is a powerful growth tool if you hear it with humility and follow it with action."

The following is an example letter, requesting feedback. You may use it as an example when you send a similar letter to those you care about, or anyone you meet that has skills, habits, or qualities you would like to implement in your own life. Warning - this can be extremely effective!

Dear _____,

As you may know, I am interested in personal growth. I would like to ask for your help in my efforts to challenge myself, learn, and improve. My relationship with you is important to me, and I want to ensure that my behavior and communication help our relationship to grow and flourish. With humility, I ask if you could take a few moments to jot down any recommendations you may have for me on this journey. How can I be a better _____ to you? How can I communicate better, or listen better?

Please know that I will read your suggestions and take them to heart. I may take a week or two to process your recommendations and think about how I can apply them to my life. Most importantly, I will honor your words and read them without judgment or frustration. I know that the best way to improve is through feedback. Your feedback is incredibly valuable to me, as I learn, grow, and improve myself. Thank you so much for being willing to support me in this endeavor!

You are helping me to be the best ME I can be!

Sincerely, _____

Affirmation:

My desire for growth is evergreen. Everyone I meet has something they can teach me. When I ask for feedback from the people I love, and those who have skills or qualities I want to implement in my own life, I accept their feedback with openness, humility, and an intense desire to be my very best self.

I am happier and exude more
joy every day.

Day 15: Negative Self-Talk to Affirmation

Stretched ☐ Sunlight ☐ Smiled ☐

My intention for today:

Today I am grateful for:

☐ Today, I will be mindfully aware of things that trigger negative reactions from me.

To Do Today:

_____

_____

_____

_____

_____

_____

_____

_____

_____

_____

_____

_____

My Torch Running Task

Morning
☐ My bedroom is a peaceful haven.

All Day
☐ My bathroom represents cleanliness & safety.

Evening
☐ My clean kitchen is a gift to my future self.

I will reach out to the following individual for networking, friendship, or mentoring:

My current financial goal & habit:

"You can create a better world for yourself through your attitude."

One of the worst habits we can have is the propensity to speak negatively to ourselves. It is self-destruction to allow yourself to believe that you are incapable of achieving your dreams and goals, that you are failing at your career, motherhood, or your marriage, or that you aren't worthy of value or love . The universe endeavored to create this perfect baby, only for her to reach adulthood and continue chiseling away at the foundations of what make her whole. THAT is what negative self talk does - it breaks our joy apart, piece by piece. You deserve so much more!

Endeavor to correct negative beliefs about yourself by destroying those thoughts that are harmful, and replacing them with words of value and encouragement.

Write down a negative belief pattern about yourself. It can be something relatively new, regarding a disappointment from the past week, or a belief you've held about yourself for many years, or even your whole life.

Examples:

I don't remember names well.
I'm a terrible housekeeper.
I never finish what I start.

Next, let's re-write that belief into something positive, even if it means the exact opposite of what we wrote before.

I remember names and faces easily.
I love keeping my home clean and entertaining unexpected visitors.
I always finish what I start. I can't wait to complete my current project so I can feel that addicting sense of accomplishment!

Read your new sentence out loud. Read it during your morning and evening routines, and keep it nearby to read during the day if you want an extra boost! I keep a running list of affirmations, or several published decks of affirmation cards handy at all times. Affirmations are an instant mood booster, a stress reliever, and a big dose of much-needed self-love.

"Be your own biggest fan, beginning today. When things get rough, that is when you need you the most!"

Here are some affirmations you may cut out and enjoy. Carry them with you in your wallet or purse, tape them to a mirror, or add them to your vision board.

I am happier and exude more joy every day.

I am 100% committed to loving life!

I can find joy in every situation.

I enjoy working toward a better ME.

I am love manifested into physical form.

My life is a continual expression of my highest joy.

By learning from masters, I can skip over pitfalls, and skyrocket toward my dreams!

Day 16: Wandering to Aiming the Arrow

Stretched ☐   Sunlight ☐   Smiled ☐

My intention for today:

Today I am grateful for:

☐ Today, I will be mindfully aware of things that trigger negative reactions from me.

☐ Today, I will notice and re-write any negative self-talk.

To Do Today:

My Torch Running Task

Morning
☐ My bedroom is a peaceful haven.

All Day
☐ My bathroom represents cleanliness & safety.

Evening
☐ My clean kitchen is a gift to my future self.

I will reach out to the following individual for networking, friendship, or mentoring:

My current financial goal & habit:

"Let your love for learning and growth be continual."

Your goals and dreams are worthy of pursuit! You deserve to utilize the best methods for goal achievement. By observing the habits, processes, and histories of mentors in your field, you can implement their methods for achieving success. Doing this puts you on the "fast track" to success, that many others miss. By following in the footsteps of giants, you can get to where you want to be.

Choose one of your goals and research a successful person in that field.

My mentor is:

Have they published any books or works that you may study?

Are there YouTube videos of them speaking or being interviewed?

How did they get to where they are today? What education, work experience, or life lessons got them to where they are?

What daily habits do they have? What is a day-in-the-life like for them?

How can you utilize what you've learned in your own life?

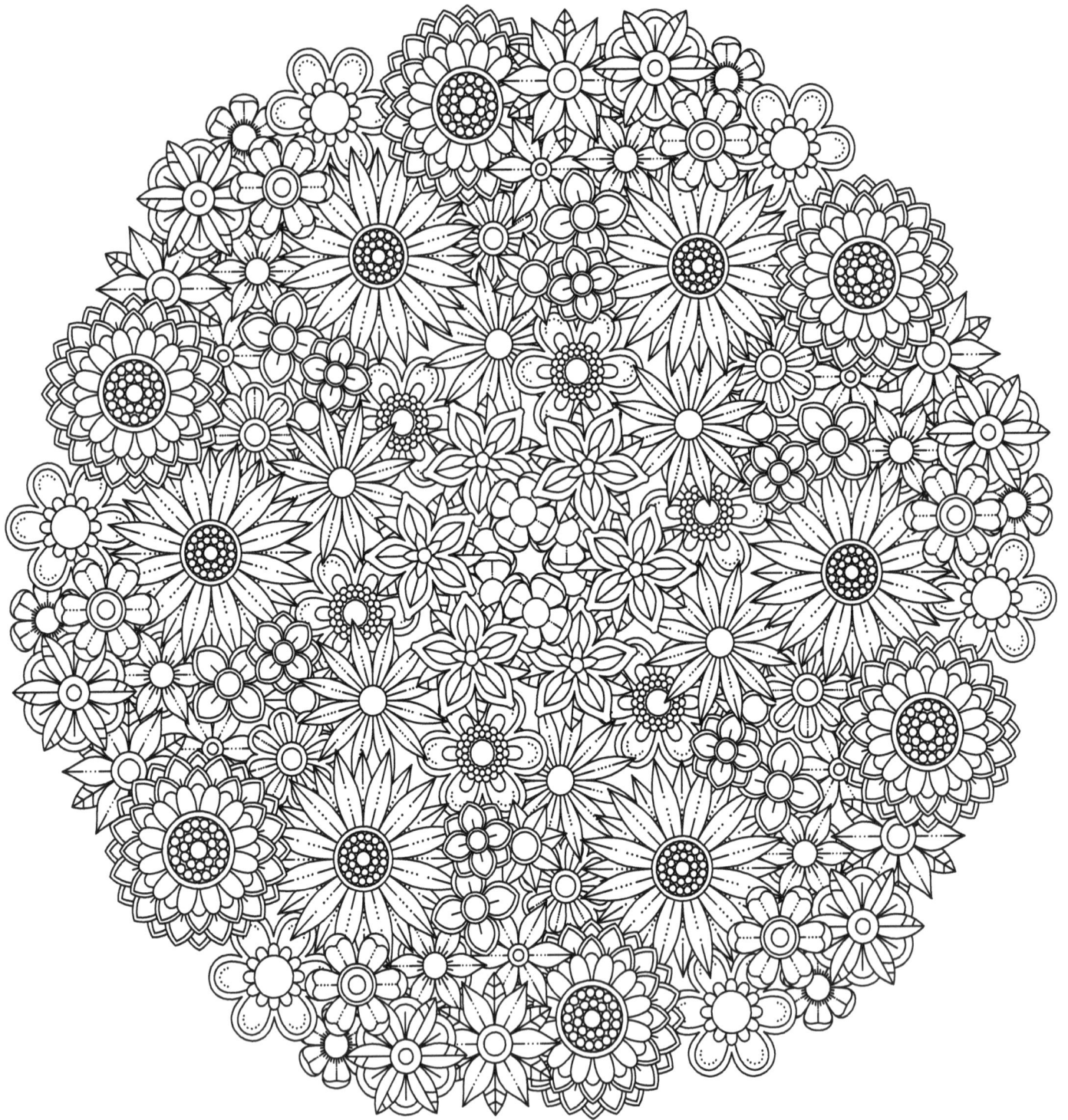

Life isn't about the destination;
it's the journey that matters.
Every small step is progress.

Day 17: Failure to Accomplishment

Stretched ☐ Sunlight ☐ Smiled ☐

My intention for today:

Today I am grateful for:

☐ Today, I will be mindfully aware of things that trigger negative reactions from me.

☐ Today, I will notice and re-write any negative self-talk.

To Do Today:

_____
_____
_____
_____
_____
_____
_____
_____
_____
_____
_____
_____
_____
_____
_____

My Torch Running Task

Morning
☐ My bedroom is a peaceful haven.

All Day
☐ My bathroom represents cleanliness & safety.

Evening
☐ My clean kitchen is a gift to my future self.

I will reach out to the following individual for networking, friendship, or mentoring:

My current financial goal & habit:

"Celebrate each level of progress and every small achievement."

Celebrating Wins

What are your top three life accomplishments?

❶

❷

❸

List three things you accomplished in the last year.

❶

❷

❸

List three things you accomplished in the last week.

❶

❷

❸

List three things as you accomplish them today. Celebrate those wins, no matter how small!

❶

❷

❸

Most of the things I worry about
will never happen.

Day 18: Worry to Courage

Stretched ☐ Sunlight ☐ Smiled ☐

My intention for today:

Today I am grateful for:

☐ Today, I will be mindfully aware of things that trigger negative reactions from me.

☐ Today, I will notice and re-write any negative self-talk.

To Do Today:

_____
_____
_____
_____
_____
_____
_____
_____
_____
_____
_____
_____
_____

My Torch Running Task

Morning
☐ My bedroom is a peaceful haven.

All Day
☐ My bathroom represents cleanliness & safety.

Evening
☐ My clean kitchen is a gift to my future self.

I will reach out to the following individual for networking, friendship, or mentoring:

My current financial goal & habit:

Wins celebrated:

"Most of the things you will worry about will never happen at all."

Alleviating Worry

Is there anything that you are worried about today?

What would be the worst-case scenario?

Is your worst fear the most likely outcome?

What actions can you take to correct, mitigate, or heal this situation?

Who can you reach out to for help or advice?

I choose to bring myself to a state of mindful awareness of the present.

Day 19: Regret to Acceptance

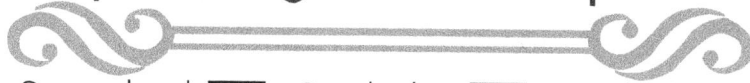

Stretched ☐ Sunlight ☐ Smiled ☐

My intention for today:

Today I am grateful for:

☐ Today, I will be mindfully aware of things that trigger negative reactions from me.

☐ Today, I will notice and re-write any negative self-talk.

To Do Today:

_____
_____
_____
_____
_____
_____
_____
_____
_____
_____
_____
_____

My Torch Running Task

Morning
☐ My bedroom is a peaceful haven.

All Day
☐ My bathroom represents cleanliness & safety.

Evening
☐ My clean kitchen is a gift to my future self.

I will reach out to the following individual for networking, friendship, or mentoring:

My current financial goal & habit:

Wins celebrated:

"Cultivate a mental attitude of wisdom, and make the best decisions you can, on a daily basis."

Learning from Regret

Are you currently struggling with regret? What event, poor choice, or missed opportunity are you thinking of?

How could that situation have been worse?

What is the silver lining from that event?

How can you avoid making that same error in judgment in the future?

"Worry and regret go hand in hand. When you worry, you're thinking about the future. When you are filled with regret, you're thinking of the past. Bringing yourself to a state of mindful awareness of the present, is essential for lasting joy."

"It's hard to learn from an experience if there is no experience to learn from."

What opportunities are waiting for you to take action, right now?

What is holding you back from taking action?

Is this something you feel led to do, or would really enjoy having in your life?

What is it costing you to postpone action on this opportunity?

"The most important change you can make right now, to reduce regret for missed opportunity, is to act. Like Nike says "Just Do It". If it won't result in death, bodily harm, divorce, or incarceration, DO IT. Take the chance that you're contemplating. Do the thing."

I am star dust! Every element that makes up the universe (and everything in it), is also present inside of me.

Day 20: A Divine Mindset

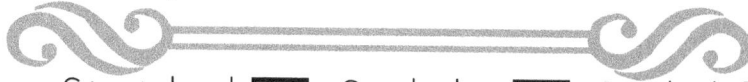

Stretched ☐ Sunlight ☐ Smiled ☐

My intention for today:

Today I am grateful for:

☐ Today, I will be mindfully aware of things that trigger negative reactions from me.

☐ Today, I will notice and re-write any negative self-talk.

To Do Today:

My Torch Running Task

Morning
☐ My bedroom is a peaceful haven.

All Day
☐ My bathroom represents cleanliness & safety.

Evening
☐ My clean kitchen is a gift to my future self.

I will reach out to the following individual for networking, friendship, or mentoring:

My current financial goal & habit:

Wins celebrated:

"Look at your situation, your body, your future and past, all through the lens of love."

❶ Fill the world with your divine Light.

Spreading your love throughout your home, your neighborhood, and indeed the whole planet and universe, is a powerful meditation that should be done on a regular basis. Through meditating on spreading our love in this way, we cultivate empathy and compassion towards all living things. We let go of self, and spend time away from our worries and regrets.

❷ Observe people, places, and opinions, through the lens of love and light.

List three people, opposing viewpoints, or other frustrations.
Take a moment to ground yourself and center your thoughts.
Then, visualize your divine love and light enveloping these subjects.
See life through their eyes, to understand and empathize.
Allow the opposition of opinion, without feelings of resentment, anger, or frustration.

❸ Visualize your ideal future, and FEEL your success!

Take a look at your goals from Day 5.
Write a short paragraph describing what life will be like for you when a particular goal is achieved. Describe it in as much detail as possible. Utilize as many of your senses as you are able. Note the way you will FEEL when you have achieved your goal. Spend a minute or two daily, holding this visualization in your mind, and feeling the emotions associated with the completion of your goal.

Mindfulness Practices

I mindfully explore the world around me, with the goal of seeing the details.

Day 21: The Minutiae

Stretched ☐ Sunlight ☐ Smiled ☐

My intention for today:

Today I am grateful for:

☐ Today, I will be mindfully aware of things that trigger negative reactions from me.

☐ Today, I will notice and re-write any negative self-talk.

To Do Today:

_____
_____
_____
_____
_____
_____
_____
_____
_____
_____
_____
_____

My Torch Running Task

Morning
☐ My bedroom is a peaceful haven.

All Day
☐ My bathroom represents cleanliness & safety.

Evening
☐ My clean kitchen is a gift to my future self.

I will reach out to the following individual for networking, friendship, or mentoring:

My current financial goal & habit:

Wins celebrated:

"Mindfully explore the world around you, with the goal of seeing the details."

Our lives are too busy. Slowing down and focusing on the minutiae around you, will separate you from the struggle of worry and regret. It will help you to quiet your mind and find the moments of "in between". In addition, when practiced regularly, focusing on small things around your residence will bring appreciation for your home and belongings.

Look around you and find one thing to really "see". Run your hands on it, feel the texture and examine the color. Imagine what the individual molecules may look like. Imagine what it may be like to run along it if you were the size of an ant. Fully devote a few minutes of your time to the space, object, or part of your home. During this time, express gratitude for whatever you are focusing upon. Enjoy it as fully as you are able.

What have you taken the time to notice today?

How did your observations create peace and calm for you?

"If you focus on one small thing per day, and wholly devote yourself to it's examination for a few minutes, it is an act of meditation."

I mindfully notice how resilient nature is, that weeds and grass continue to peek between sidewalk slabs and driveway cracks.

Day 22: Green Growth

Stretched ☐ Sunlight ☐ Smiled ☐

My intention for today:

Today I am grateful for:

☐ Today, I will be mindfully aware of things that trigger negative reactions from me.

☐ Today, I will notice and re-write any negative self-talk.

To Do Today:

_____
_____
_____
_____
_____
_____
_____
_____
_____
_____
_____

My Torch Running Task

Morning
☐ My bedroom is a peaceful haven.

All Day
☐ My bathroom represents cleanliness & safety.

Evening
☐ My clean kitchen is a gift to my future self.

I will reach out to the following individual for networking, friendship, or mentoring:

My current financial goal & habit:

Wins celebrated:

"Nature plays a large role in the morale of human beings."

It's time to get dirty! Go outside. If you can, get your bare feet on the grass, dirt, or sand. Take a moment to feel the sunshine on your skin. Done daily, a short walk in nature will give you a boost of creativity and concentration, and uplift your mood. So go play!

Journal about your experiences today below:

Press a leaf, flower, or other natural artifact, or place a photograph or sketch from your experience here.

Happiness is contagious, and
it's effects are lasting.

Day 23: Fellowship

Stretched ☐ Sunlight ☐ Smiled ☐

My intention for today:

Today I am grateful for:

☐ Today, I will be mindfully aware of things that trigger negative reactions from me.

☐ Today, I will notice and re-write any negative self-talk.

To Do Today:

My Torch Running Task

Morning
☐ My bedroom is a peaceful haven.

All Day
☐ My bathroom represents cleanliness & safety.

Evening
☐ My clean kitchen is a gift to my future self.

I will reach out to the following individual for networking, friendship, or mentoring:

My current financial goal & habit:

Wins celebrated:

"Happiness is contagious, and it's effects are lasting."

When was the last time you hosted a meal, party, game, or movie night? If it's been awhile, now is the time to take the initiative and get some much-needed fellowship.

Use the following page to plan a gathering with friends or family. Keep the food simple, easy to prepare and suitable for your guests. Don't put too much pressure on yourself! Plan some fun and games, or a simple conversational round-table.

Even something as simple as lunch out with your bestie, or tea with a few of the neighbors, will do wonders for your mood. Spending time with others can also be a mindful exercise in loving acceptance of differing opinions. Take advantage of any time spent with others to cultivate empathy and compassion.

Write a short thank-you note, get well, or condolence, to send to someone in the mail. Keep cards for various occasions handy, and make note of the birth dates, anniversaries, and other important dates of those whom you meet and regularly engage with.

Person's Name:

Type of correspondence to send:

Sent ☐

Person's Name:

Type of correspondence to send:

Sent ☐

Person's Name:

Type of correspondence to send:

Sent ☐

Fellonship Planning

Occasion/Theme_____   Budget_____

Who	
What	
Where	
When	

Food/Beverages:

Decorations:

Invitations/Favors:

Seating/Table Setting:

The feeling of being needed is one of the fundamental ingredients to reducing depression.

Day 24: Animal Snuggles

Stretched ☐ Sunlight ☐ Smiled ☐

My intention for today:

Today I am grateful for:

☐ Today, I will be mindfully aware of things that trigger negative reactions from me.

☐ Today, I will notice and re-write any negative self-talk.

To Do Today:

_____
_____
_____
_____
_____
_____
_____
_____
_____
_____

My Torch Running Task

Morning
☐ My bedroom is a peaceful haven.

All Day
☐ My bathroom represents cleanliness & safety.

Evening
☐ My clean kitchen is a gift to my future self.

I will reach out to the following individual for networking, friendship, or mentoring:

My current financial goal & habit:

Wins celebrated:

"The feeling of being needed is one of the fundamental ingredients to reducing depression."

Journal here regarding your experiences with pet ownership or care. If you have a pet, describe how they benefit you or your family. If you do not currently have a pet that you can hold, snuggle, or pet, think about how you might be able to spend time with an animal. What benefits might you gain? Record your thoughts on what your ideal pet might be, and how you might care for them and spend time with them.

"Pets are sensitive to human emotions, and can tell when someone needs a bit of laughter, or when they need gentle comforting instead."

I may plan for my life's journey from point A to point B in a straight line, but life is full of unexpected twists and turns.

Day 25: The Winds of Change

Stretched ☐ Sunlight ☐ Smiled ☐

My intention for today:

Today I am grateful for:

☐ Today, I will be mindfully aware of things that trigger negative reactions from me.

☐ Today, I will notice and re-write any negative self-talk.

To Do Today:

_____
_____
_____
_____
_____
_____
_____
_____
_____
_____
_____
_____

My Torch Running Task

Morning
☐ My bedroom is a peaceful haven.

All Day
☐ My bathroom represents cleanliness & safety.

Evening
☐ My clean kitchen is a gift to my future self.

I will reach out to the following individual for networking, friendship, or mentoring:

My current financial goal & habit:

Wins celebrated:

"Imagine the light from your being filling the space you're sitting in right now."

Accepting Change

What recent change have you struggled with?

Is there any part of this change that you can prevent, alter to your advantage, or modify?

What parts of this change are completely out of your control? Use your mindfulness practice to let go of those things you cannot change.

Ask yourself "How can I approach this situation with grace and mindfulness?"

Is there a friend or family member struggling with change? In what ways can you assist them in their struggle to accept those changes?

Water focuses your thoughts
with a rhythm and gentle flow
that is meditative.

Day 26: Flowing Waters

Stretched ☐ Sunlight ☐ Smiled ☐

My intention for today:

Today I am grateful for:

☐ Today, I will be mindfully aware of things that trigger negative reactions from me.

☐ Today, I will notice and re-write any negative self-talk.

To Do Today:

My Torch Running Task

Morning
☐ My bedroom is a peaceful haven.

All Day
☐ My bathroom represents cleanliness & safety.

Evening
☐ My clean kitchen is a gift to my future self.

I will reach out to the following individual for networking, friendship, or mentoring:

My current financial goal & habit:

Wins celebrated:

"Water evokes feelings of happiness and satisfaction, calm, peace, and unity."

The link between water and stress reduction is well documented. Just the act of drinking a single 8oz glass of water can reduce cortisol (stress hormone) levels considerably.

Listening to running water is calming, rhythmic, and meditative. If you are an artist or writer, if you are in need of problem solving or creative thought, taking time to think near a flowing water source is a relaxing way to get the answers you need, or spark insight and creativity.

Take some time to mindfully experience one of the most abundant resources of our planet. Visit bodies of water, sit in the park next to a stream, and renew your appreciation for water while bathing.

Ways to enjoy water mindfully:
- Express gratitude for your clean drinking water - so many on the planet do not have this.
- Close your eyes while you wash your hands, concentrating on the soothing feel of the water on your skin.
- Take time to listen to water running or falling.
- Run your hands or feet in a natural water source.
- Swim in a lake or in the ocean.
- Listen to waves crash upon the shore.
- Watch a stream or river from a bridge over it.
- Bathe quietly, with the intention of simply enjoying the water.

Journal some of your mindful water experiences below:

_____

_____

_____

_____

_____

_____

Conquering my fears
empowers me to enjoy life as
I was meant to!

Day 27: Crawlies Aren't All Creepy

Stretched ☐ Sunlight ☐ Smiled ☐

My intention for today:

Today I am grateful for:

☐ Today, I will be mindfully aware of things that trigger negative reactions from me.

☐ Today, I will notice and re-write any negative self-talk.

To Do Today:

My Torch Running Task

Morning
☐ My bedroom is a peaceful haven.

All Day
☐ My bathroom represents cleanliness & safety.

Evening
☐ My clean kitchen is a gift to my future self.

I will reach out to the following individual for networking, friendship, or mentoring:

My current financial goal & habit:

Wins celebrated:

"Conquering your fears empowers you to enjoy life as you were meant to!"

Are there any creatures, places, events, or situations that cause you trepidation and fear?

If so, why do you think you feel this way?

How can you educate yourself more about this thing to reduce your fear of it?

Take action today and learn something new about anything that is causing you to feel fear. Allow your newfound knowledge to cleanse away your fear of it. As long as the fear remains, continue to educate yourself as much as you are able.

Journal your self-education below:

Be encouraged. Some fears are so strong that professional help is needed to completely understand our feelings and to alleviate the burden that phobias can have on us.

Food is fuel for my body.
Everything I ingest contributes to
my health or disease.

Day 28: A Cuppa

Stretched ☐ Sunlight ☐ Smiled ☐

My intention for today:

Today I am grateful for:

☐ Today, I will be mindfully aware of things that trigger negative reactions from me.

☐ Today, I will notice and re-write any negative self-talk.

To Do Today:

_____
_____
_____
_____
_____
_____
_____
_____
_____
_____
_____
_____

My Torch Running Task

Morning
☐ My bedroom is a peaceful haven.

All Day
☐ My bathroom represents cleanliness & safety.

Evening
☐ My clean kitchen is a gift to my future self.

I will reach out to the following individual for networking, friendship, or mentoring:

My current financial goal & habit:

Wins celebrated:

"Food is fuel for our bodies. Everything you ingest contributes to your health or disease."

It's time for an exercise in mindful drinking. Choose a drink, hot or cool. Find a quiet spot and *just* drink. Let the world slip away as you wholly devote your time to consuming the liquid, and nothing else. You may simply relax and enjoy the time as a way to fill your internal "cup". Or, you may wish to meditate upon the origin of the liquid and all it's ingredients. Where do the coffee beans, tea leaves, or cocoa beans come from? Who's hands have made your drink possible? What deep well, spring, or tall mountain snow-melt brought the water to you?

Journal your experience here:

_____
_____
_____
_____
_____
_____
_____
_____
_____
_____
_____
_____
_____

"Do you drink a glass of water when you first wake, knowing that you are most dehydrated after a night's rest?"

I am mindfully aware of all
that is around me.

Day 29: A Good Meal

Stretched ☐ Sunlight ☐ Smiled ☐

My intention for today:

Today I am grateful for:

☐ Today, I will be mindfully aware of things that trigger negative reactions from me.

☐ Today, I will notice and re-write any negative self-talk.

To Do Today:

_____
_____
_____
_____
_____
_____
_____
_____
_____
_____
_____

My Torch Running Task

Morning
☐ My bedroom is a peaceful haven.

All Day
☐ My bathroom represents cleanliness & safety.

Evening
☐ My clean kitchen is a gift to my future self.

I will reach out to the following individual for networking, friendship, or mentoring:

My current financial goal & habit:

Wins celebrated:

"Slow down when you eat. Especially when taking the very first bite."

Mindful Food Journal

Date_____

Breakfast	Experience

Lunch	Experience

Supper	Experience

I am an ambassador for mindful, loving touch; sharing my light and love with all those I come in contact with.

Day 30: The Healing Power of Touch

Stretched ☐ Sunlight ☐ Smiled ☐

My intention for today:

Today I am grateful for:

☐ Today, I will be mindfully aware of things that trigger negative reactions from me.

☐ Today, I will notice and re-write any negative self-talk.

To Do Today:

_____
_____
_____
_____
_____
_____
_____
_____
_____
_____

My Torch Running Task

Morning
☐ My bedroom is a peaceful haven.

All Day
☐ My bathroom represents cleanliness & safety.

Evening
☐ My clean kitchen is a gift to my future self.

I will reach out to the following individual for networking, friendship, or mentoring:

My current financial goal & habit:

Wins celebrated:

"A hug costs nothing, but is priceless!"

Seek out and give hugs. Sneak light touches in whenever you pass by a loved one. Shake hands with strangers, teachers, and government workers. Giving these people a bit of human contact will boost their mood, increase their serotonin levels and promote an instant relationship boost between you.

With whom did you interact with mindful, loving touch today?

In what ways do you feel you can increase your human touch contact with the others in your family, or with strangers?

"Human touch causes a decrease in violence, improves trust, cooperation, and teamwork; and increases intimacy. Our health, happiness, and wellbeing improve when we're regularly touched by another person."

Congratulations!

You are amazing!

I'm so proud of you for all you have accomplished. This companion workbook has been a labor of love and personal growth for me. So much so, that I am pleased and proud to encourage others to complete the same journey.

Know thyself.

Moving forward, remember to be mindful. Notice things around you. Continue asking yourself questions and discovering who you are, what you believe, and who you want to be. While you grow, I encourage you to remember that you are already perfect, just as you are.

With so much love my heart would burst,
Janeen

Resources

Unleash Joy: 30 Days to Clarity, Peace, and Long-Awaited Happiness
    May be found on Amazon, Barns and Noble, and wherever books are sold.

For coaching availability inquiries, and articles written by the author, see her website at:

www.JaneenBrown.com

For other helpful resources and products, including my FREE Emergency Bad Day Survival Guide, see:

www.UnleashJoy.com/resources